VISIONS

KNITTING
MEETS
ART

15 designs by Jen Geigley

Photography by Joelle Blanchard

Design & Pattern Writing | Jen Geigley
Photography | Joelle Blanchard
Design, Layout & Illustrations | Jen Geigley
Models | Joelle Blanchard, Nyayop Chuol Toang, Armin Trepic
Technical Editing | Stefanie Goodwin-Ritter
Sample Knitting | Nichole McDowell
Location | Des Moines Social Club, Des Moines, Iowa

Visions: Knitting Meets Art

Wholesale Ordering Information
Deep South Fibers
www.deepsouthfibers.com

ISBN-13: 978-1981756261
ISBN-10: 1981756264

MOON PHASE PUBLICATIONS
www.MoonPhasePublications.com

CRA015000
Crafts & Hobbies | Needlework | Knitting

10 9 8 7 6 5 4 3 2 1

C O N T E N T S

To Steven Mark Berg. StevenBe, the glitter knitter with a passion for fashion. You have been a tremendous influence to me creatively as a knitting rebel, rule breaker and statement maker. Thank you for your kindness and support; thank you for being an inspiration and a friend.

INTRODUCTION

Why do knitters knit? Maybe we have a simple desire to make our own clothing and accessories. Maybe it's a way to express ourselves. The yarns we choose, the color palettes we are drawn to, the modifications we make … this is how we play and create. Using skill and creativity, craftsmanship and ideas, a knitter can make almost anything. We create clothing and accessories that can't be bought or found anywhere else. We are conscious beings, not machines. We make tiny mistakes and sometimes our tension isn't perfect, but in the end we create something that is uniquely ours. And that's such a beautiful thing.

A ball of yarn can be transformed into just about anything in the hands of a knitter, and in this book I hope to show you how your knitted fabric can become your canvas.

True to my rebel heart, sometimes I feel the need to let go, break the rules and embrace the unexpected. To express myself freely. I cannot explain to you the joy I felt creating the pieces in this collection. Spreading them out on newspapers and flinging paint and bleach in an intentional, yet very careless, arbitrary way. I can't wait to share this with you.

Many knits in this book were altered in some way after the knitting process was complete and some were left untouched. But this book is written for every knitter. The dyeing, bleaching and painting techniques are optional. Each piece in this collection can be knitted and left as-is, or you can take it a step further and used mixed media to create something brand new. I will show you how with techniques explained at the end of this book. And never fear – you will be using swatches to test the different outcomes of your artistic experiments before you decide to dip-dye or hand-paint your knits. I dare you to try something new. I don't believe in mistakes. Trust your creativity and let your knits become what they want to be.

– Jen Geigley

POLAR
SUPER BULKY THROW
PAGE 101

BLEACH
BLEACHED BANDANA
PAGE 103

GLACIER
DIP-DYED PULLOVER
PAGE 104

HUNTER
COWL
PAGE 107

The Book Cellar

47 36-38 N Lincoln Ave
Chicago, IL 60625
(773) 293-2665

No cash refunds. Store credit only within 15
days, with receipt.

Cust: **Mullins, Heidi**

06-Jan-20 7:08p   Clerk:book
Trns. # 10634501   Reg: 1

978198175626 1	*Visions: Knitting Me*	
1 @ $27.00	-10.0	$24.30
9781454711087	*Edwards Menagerie Th*	
1 @ $19.95	-10.0	$17.96

	Sub-total:	$46.95
	Tax @ 10.250%:	$4.33
	Discount:	$4.69
	Total:	**$46.59**

* *Non-Tax Items*
  Items 2   *Units 2*

Payment Via:

VISA/MC/Discover $46.59

HALO
COWL WRAP
PAGE 108

TWIG
HAT
PAGE 110

SPACE
STRIPED COWL
PAGE 113

ECHO
SPLATTER PAINTED COWL
PAGE 112

SPACE
COWL
PAGE 113

ECHO
COWL
PAGE 112

LINK
COWL
PAGE 114

CLOUD
SUPER SCARF
PAGE 121

CALIFORNIA
HAT
PAGE 122

CALIFORNIA
HAT
PAGE 122

REBEL
HANDPAINTED TANK
PAGE 126

Windows

DESIGN NOTES

Windows is a bottom-up raglan worked seamless in the round with side slits along the bottom edge and 2 inches of positive ease. The pattern shown here was stamped with the bristles of a large paintbrush using white fabric paint. Find paint and stamping instructions in the 'Dye, Bleach and Paint Techniques' section on page 130 of this book.

SIZES

To Fit Bust: 34 (36, 38, 40, 42, 44, 46, 50, 52, 54) inches

FINISHED BUST MEASUREMENT

36 (38, 40, 42, 44, 46, 48, 52, 54, 56) inches

YARN

Ewe Ewe Baa Baa Bulky in Black Licorice (Bulky, 100% fine merino wool; 132 yards per 100 g skein)

6 (6, 7, 7, 8, 9, 10, 11, 12, 13) skeins

792 (792, 924, 924, 1056, 1188, 1320, 1452, 1584, 1716) yards

Note: It is always advisable to purchase an extra 'safety' skein of yarn.

NEEDLES

US 10 (6 mm) 24 in circular needles and/or 8 in double pointed needles
(or size needed to obtain gauge)

NOTIONS

Stitch markers (3 in one color, 1 in contrast color)
Tapestry needle

GAUGE

4 inches = 16 sts and 20 rows in St st on US 10 (6 mm) needles

STITCH GUIDE

Single Rib (flat):
Row 1: Sl 1, *k1, p1, rep from * last stitch of row, k1.
Row 2: Sl 1, *k1, p1, rep from * to last stitch of row, k1.

Single Rib (in the round):
All rnds: *K1, p1, rep from *.

Stockinette Stitch (flat):
Row 1 (RS): Sl 1, k all sts.
Row 2 (WS): Sl 1, p all sts.

Stockinette Stitch (in the round):
All rnds: K all sts.

ABBREVIATIONS

CO - cast on
BO - bind off
k – knit
st(s) - stitch(es)
rnd - round
beg – beginning
dec - decrease
inc – increase
meas - measures
p - purl
pm - place marker
rep - repeat
rnd - round
st st - stockinette stitch
sl – slip (as if to purl)
sm – slip marker
kfb - knit into the front and back of the same stitch
(one stitch increased)

DIRECTIONS

FRONT
Using long-tail method and US 10 (6 mm) needles, CO 72 (76, 80, 84, 88, 92, 96, 100, 104, 108) sts.
Work in Single Rib Stitch (flat) for 10 rows total, then work in Stockinette Stitch (flat) until piece measures 6 in from CO edge, ending on a purl row. Break yarn.

BACK
Using long-tail method and US 10 (6 mm) needles, CO 72 (76, 80, 84, 88, 92, 96, 100, 104, 108) sts.
Slipping first st of each row, work in Single Rib Stitch (flat) for 10 rows total, then work in Stockinette Stitch (flat) until piece measures 6 in from CO edge, ending on a purl row.

With RS facing, join Front and Back sts to work in the round, pm to mark the beginning of the round.

Work in Stockinette Stitch in the round until piece measures 15 (15, 15, 15, 15, 16, 16, 16, 17, 17) inches from CO edge, ending last rnd 4 (4, 4, 4, 4, 6, 6, 6, 6, 6) sts before marker.

*BO 8 (8, 8, 8, 8, 12, 12, 12, 12, 12) sts, k 64 (68, 72, 76, 80, 80, 84, 88, 92, 96) sts, repeat from *. You will have 64 (68, 72, 76, 80, 80, 84, 88, 92, 96) sts for both the front and back. Set aside.

SLEEVES
Using Magic Loop or DPNs, CO 38 (38, 40, 40, 40, 44, 44, 44, 46, 46) sts, pm and join in the round, being careful not to twist sts.

Work in Single Rib Stitch for 10 rnds total.

Begin working Stockinette Stitch (in the round), working increases as follows:

Increase Round: K1, m1, knit all sts in rnd to marker, m1. 40 (40, 42, 42, 42, 46, 46, 46, 48, 48) sts.

Work Increase Round every 6 rnds 0 (0, 0, 3, 1, 5, 5, 6, 10, 13) more times. 40 (40, 42, 48, 44, 56, 56, 58, 68, 74) sts.

Work Increase Round every 8 rnds 7 (8, 9, 7, 9, 6, 6, 6, 3, 1) more times. 54 (56, 60, 62, 62, 68, 68, 70, 74, 76) sts.

Work until sleeve measures 17 (17, 17, 17, 18, 18, 19, 19, 20, 20) inches from CO edge, ending 4 (4, 4, 4, 4, 6, 6, 6, 6, 6) sts before marker.

BO next 8 (8, 8, 8, 8, 12, 12, 12, 12, 12) sts, work to end of rnd. 46 (48, 52, 54, 54, 56, 56, 58, 62, 64) sts.

Set aside, make second sleeve the same as the first.

With right sides facing, join sleeves to body as follows:

K across 46 (48, 52, 54, 54, 56, 56, 58, 62, 64) left sleeve sts, pm, k across first 32 (34, 36, 38, 40, 40, 42, 44, 46, 48) front sts, place unique marker for center front, k across second 32 (34, 36, 38, 40, 40, 42, 44, 46, 48) front sts, pm, k across 46 (48, 52, 54, 54, 56, 56, 58, 62, 64) right sleeve sts, pm, k across 64 (68, 72, 76, 80, 80, 84, 88, 92, 96) back sts, place contrasting m for end of the rnd. 220 (232, 248, 260, 268, 272, 280, 292, 308, 320) sts.

RAGLAN
Note: you will need to ignore the unique marker placed for center front when working Decrease Round below, until noted.
Decrease Round: *K2tog, k to 2 sts before next marker, ssk, slip marker, rep from * 3 more times. (8 sts dec)

Work 1 round even.

Work Decrease Round every 2 rnds 15 (16, 17, 18, 19, 19, 20, 20, 21, 21) more times. 92 (96, 104, 108, 108, 112, 112, 124, 132, 144) sts.

Next Round: BO center front sts by working in established pattern to 5 (5, 5, 5, 6, 6, 6, 6, 7, 7) sts before unique center front marker, then BO next 10 (10, 10, 12, 12, 12, 12, 12, 14, 14) sts (remove unique marker), knit to end of round, then continue knitting across left sleeve and front stitches to center front. 82 (86, 94, 96, 96, 100, 100, 112, 118, 130) sts.

You will now begin working Stockinette Stitch (flat) beginning with a WS row as follows:

Neck Dec. Row 1 (WS): BO 3 sts, purl to end of row. 79 (83, 91, 93, 93, 97, 97, 109, 115, 127) sts.

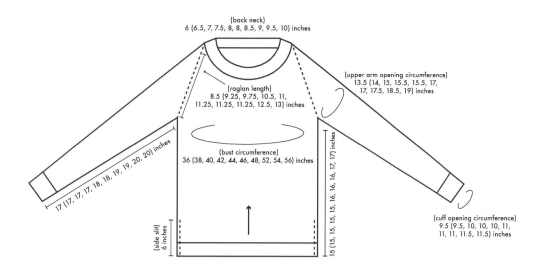

(back neck)
6 (6.5, 7, 7.5, 8, 8, 8.5, 9, 9.5, 10) inches

(upper arm opening circumference)
13.5 (14, 15, 15.5, 15.5, 17, 17, 17.5, 18.5, 19) inches

(raglan length)
8.5 (9.25, 9.75, 10.5, 11, 11.25, 11.25, 11.25, 12.5, 13) inches

(bust circumference)
36 (38, 40, 42, 44, 46, 48, 52, 54, 56) inches

15 (15, 15, 15, 16, 16, 16, 17, 17) inches

17 (17, 17, 17, 18, 19, 19, 20, 20) inches

(side slit)
6 inches

(cuff opening circumference)
9.5 (9.5, 10, 10, 10, 11, 11, 11, 11.5, 11.5) inches

Neck & Raglan Dec. Row 2 (RS): BO 3 sts, k to 2 sts before next marker, ssk, slip marker, *K2tog, k to 2 sts before next marker, ssk, slip marker, rep from * 3 more times, k to end of row. 68 (72, 80, 82, 82, 86, 86, 98, 104, 116) sts.

Neck Dec. Row 3 (WS): BO 2 sts, purl to end of row. 66 (70, 78, 80, 80, 84, 84, 96, 102, 114) sts.

Neck & Raglan Dec. Row 4 (RS): BO 2 sts, k to 2 sts before next marker, ssk, slip marker, *K2tog, k to 2 sts before next marker, ssk, slip marker, rep from * 3 more times, k to end of row. 56 (60, 68, 70, 70, 74, 74, 86, 92, 104) sts.

All Sizes: Repeat Rows 3 & 4 1 (1, 1, 2, 1, 1, 1, 2, 2, 3) more times. 44 (48, 56, 46, 58, 62, 62, 62, 62, 68, 68) sts.

Neck Dec. Row 5 (WS): BO 1 st, purl to end of row. 43 (47, 55, 45, 57, 61, 61, 61, 67, 67) sts.

Neck & Raglan Dec. Row 6 (RS): BO 1 st, k to 2 sts before next marker, ssk, slip marker, *K2tog, k to 2 sts before next marker, ssk, slip marker, rep from * 3 more times, k to end of row. 34 (38, 46, 36, 48, 52, 56, 52, 58, 58) sts.

Neck Dec. Row 7 (WS): BO 1 sts, purl to end of row. 33 (37, 45, 35, 47, 51, 51, 51, 57, 57) sts.

Neck Dec. Row 8 (RS): BO 1 st, k to end of row. 32 (36, 44, 34, 46, 50, 50, 50, 56, 56) sts.

Repeat Rows 7 & 8 0 (1, 0, 2, 2, 3, 2, 1, 3, 3) more times. 32 (34, 44, 30, 42, 44, 46, 48, 50, 50) sts rem.

BO all sts.

BLOCKING
Soak using your favorite no-rinse wash in lukewarm water for 15-20 minutes, gently lay garment out and shape. Dry flat.

FINISHING
Sew underarm seams.

CREWNECK NECKBAND
Starting at shoulder with smaller needle and RS facing, PU and knit approximately 30 (32, 32, 34, 36, 42, 44, 46, 46, 48) sts. Join in the round and PM. Work in Single Rib (in the round) for 8 rounds. BO loosely, in pattern.

Polar

DESIGN NOTES
You'll fall in love with this throw knitted using the most luxurious, soft, humongous yarn from Knit Safari. This smooth, tubular yarn is like no other and will not fray, fuzz or pill. Get cozy.

SIZES
One size

FINISHED MEASUREMENTS
35 inches wide and 50 inches long

YARN
Knit Safari Jumbo Yarn in Dove Grey (Super Bulky, 70% Polyamide, 30% Cotton; approx. 26 yards per 200 g ball) 10 balls (260 yards)

NEEDLES
US 50 (25 mm) 32" - 40" circular needles (or size needed to obtain gauge)

NOTIONS
Sewing needle and matching thread (for sewing ends of yarn together)

GAUGE
4 inches = 3 sts and 5 rows in Stockinette Stitch on size 50 (25 mm) needles, unblocked

STITCH GUIDE
Stockinette Stitch:
Row 1 (RS): K all sts.
Row 2 (WS): P all sts.

Seed Stitch
Row 1 (RS): *k1, p1, rep from * to end of row.
Row 2 (WS): *p1, k1, rep from * to end of row.

ABBREVIATIONS
Approx. - approximate
CO - cast on
BO - bind off
k – knit
p - purl
RS - right side
st(s) - stitch(es)
WS - wrong side

DIRECTIONS
Using long-tail method on US 50 needles, CO 25 sts.

Slipping first st of each row, work in Stockinette Stitch until you have used 2 balls of yarn (approx. 10 inches).

Slipping first st of each row, work in Seed Stitch until you have used 2 balls of yarn (approx. 10 inches).

Repeat these two steps until you have used all 10 balls of yarn, leaving enough yarn to BO.

BO all sts in pattern, loosely.

JOINING ENDS
Squish ends until they are a uniform shape. Trim any loose threads. Using a sewing needle and matching thread, use small stitches to sew the two ends of the tubes together, working around the outside perimeter. Sew around the tube twice, making sure seam is secure. Tie a knot, trim thread. Squish again to reshape and continue knitting.

FINISHING
Cut yarn, leaving a 6 inch tail. Using your fingers, tuck in ends.

BLOCKING
Blocking is unnecessary.

Bleach

DESIGN NOTES
Knit from point to flat edge, this shawl is a work of art once you add bleach. I highly recommend using the yarn suggested below (Rowan Denim) because it's the only yarn I've found that bleaches to pure white. Find detailed bleach instructions in the 'Dye, Bleach and Paint Techniques' section on page 130 of this book.

SIZES
One size

FINISHED MEASUREMENTS (after blocking)
20 inches tall and 52 inches wide

YARN
Rowan Denim in Black (DK; 100% Cotton; 98 yds per 50 g ball)
5 balls
490 yards

NEEDLES
US 6 (4 mm) 40 inch circular needles
(or size needed to obtain gauge)

NOTIONS
Stitch markers (2)
Tapestry needle

GAUGE
4 inches = 17 sts and 32 rows in Stockinette Stitch on US 6 (4 mm) needles

STITCH GUIDE
Garter Stitch (flat):
Row 1 (RS): Knit.
Row 2 (WS): Knit.

ABBREVIATIONS
CO - cast on
BO - bind off
k – knit
st(s) - stitch(es)
m - marker
m1l - make one left
m1r - make one right
p - purl
pm - place marker
RS - right side
sl - slip
WS - wrong side

DIRECTIONS
Using long-tail method on US 6 needles, CO 7 sts.

Set up rows:
First row (WS): K3, pm, p1, pm, k3.
Next row (RS): K3, m1l, sl m, k1, sl m, m1r, k3. 9 sts (2 sts increased).
Next row (WS): K3, p3, k3.

Row 1 (RS): K3, m1l, k to m, m1r, sl m, k1, sl m, m1l, k to last 3 sts, m1r, k3. 13 sts (4 sts increased).

Row 2 (WS:) K3, p to last 3 sts, k3.

Repeat rows 1 and 2 a total of 68 times - 281 sts.

Piece should measure approximately 19 inches from CO edge. You can also opt to repeat these last 2 rows until you reach your length desired.205 sts.

Work in Garter Stitch for 3 rows.

BO very loosely, using needle one size up if you wish.

FINISHING
Cut yarn, leaving a 6-8 inch tail. Using tapestry needle, weave in ends.

BLEACHING (optional)
If you choose to bleach your bandana, do so before blocking. Cover your work area to protect surface underneath (or work outdoors.) Use a paintbrush to splatter bleach onto your garment, or drip small amounts using a small container or the cap of the bleach bottle. Find detailed bleach tips on page 130 of this book.

BLOCKING
Soak garment in bowl of lukewarm water and a few drops of no-rinse fabric wash. Gently wring out and lay garment on a towel and use towel to remove excess water. Lay out garment and shape to desired shape and dimensions. Allow to dry completely.

Glacier

DESIGN NOTES
Glacier is a unisex top-down raglan worked seamless in the round and fits like your favorite sweatshirt. White Spud & Chloë Outer yarn was used to knit this pullover, then it was dipped in black dye to create a gradient. Find detailed dyeing instructions in the 'Dye, Bleach and Paint Techniques' section on page 130 of this book.

SIZES
34 (36, 38, 40, 42, 44, 46, 48, 50, 52)

To Fit Bust: 34 (36, 38, 40, 42, 44, 46, 48, 50, 52) inches

FINISHED MEASUREMENTS (after blocking)
34 (36, 38, 40, 42, 44, 46, 48, 50, 52) inches

YARN
Spud & Chloë Outer by Blue Sky Fibers in Snow Day (Bulky; 65% Superwash Wool/35% Organic Cotton; 60 yards per 100g skein)
9 (9, 10, 10, 11, 12, 12, 13, 14, 15) skeins
540 (540, 600, 600, 660, 720, 720, 780, 840, 900) yards

NEEDLES
US 11 (8 mm) 24" circular needles (or size needed to obtain gauge)
US 11 (8 mm) 8 in double pointed needles (or size needed to obtain gauge)

NOTIONS
Stitch markers (3 in one color, 1 in contrast color)
Stitch holders or scrap yarn
Tapestry needle

GAUGE
4 inches = 9 sts and 12 rnds in Stockinette Stitch on US 13 needles

STITCH GUIDE
Stockinette Stitch (in the round)
K all sts.

Single Rib (in the round):
All rnds: *K1, p1, rep from *.

ABBREVIATIONS
CO - cast on
BO - bind off
k – knit
k2tog - knit 2 sts together (1 st decreased)
inc – increase
m - marker
m1r – make one right (pick up the bar between the stitch you've knitted and the one you're about to knit from back to front, knit through the front of new loop)
m1l – make one left (pick up the bar between the stitch you've knitted and the one you're about to knit from front to back, knit through the back of new loop)
p - purl
pm - place marker
rep - repeat
rnd(s) - round(s)
RS - right side
st(s) - stitch(es)
sl – slip
ssk - slip, slip, knit these two stitches together (1 st decreased)
WS - wrong side

DIRECTIONS

Using long-tail method and US 11 needles, CO 20 (20, 22, 22, 24, 28, 30, 30, 32, 32) sts. Do not join; work flat.

Set-up Row (WS): P1, pm, p3 (3, 3, 3, 3, 3, 4, 4, 4, 4), pm, p 12 (12, 14, 14, 18, 16, 20, 20, 22, 22) pm, p3 (3, 3, 3, 3, 3, 4, 4, 4, 4), pm, p 1 st.

Raglan Increases

Next Row (RS inc): K1, m1r, knit to first marker, sl m, *k1, m1l, k to 1 st before marker, m1r, k1, sl m;rep from * 2 more times, k to 1 st before end of row, m1l, k1. 8 sts increased. 28 (28, 30, 30, 32, 36, 38, 38, 40, 40) sts.

Next Row (WS): P across.

Repeat these 2 rnds 9 (8, 8, 9, 10, 8, 9, 10, 11, 12) more times.

Repeat increase rnd every 4 rnds 1 (3, 3, 3, 5, 3, 5, 5, 5, 5) more times.

AT THE SAME TIME: After working 4 rows, CO 1 st at each end of needle for neck edge. (2 sts inc).

Next Row: CO 2 sts at each end of needle. (4 sts inc).

Next RS Row: CO 4 (6, 8, 8, 6, 8, 8, 8, 6, 6) sts at center front. Join in round, taking care not to twist sts. 118 (128, 132, 140, 148, 154, 164, 172, 180,188) sts.

34 (38, 40, 42, 42, 44, 46, 48, 48, 50) front sts; 25 (27, 27, 29, 31, 32, 34, 36, 38, 40) right sleeve sts; 34 (36, 38, 40, 44, 46, 50, 52, 56, 58) back sts; 25 (27, 27, 29, 31, 32, 34, 36, 38, 40) left sleeve sts.

Work 34 (36, 38, 40, 44, 46, 50, 52, 56, 58) sts for back, then place next 25 (27, 27, 29, 31, 32, 34, 36, 38, 40) sts on holder for right sleeve; CO 4 sts, work 34 (38, 40, 42, 42, 44, 46, 48, 48, 50) sts (front), place next 25 (27, 27, 29, 31, 32, 34, 36, 38, 40) sts on holder for left sleeve; CO 4 sts. 76 (82, 86, 90, 94, 98, 104, 108, 112, 116) sts rem.

Work in Stockinette Stitch until piece measures 18 (18, 18, 19, 19, 19, 20, 20, 20, 20) inches from underarm.

Work in Single Rib for 7 rnds.

BO all sts.

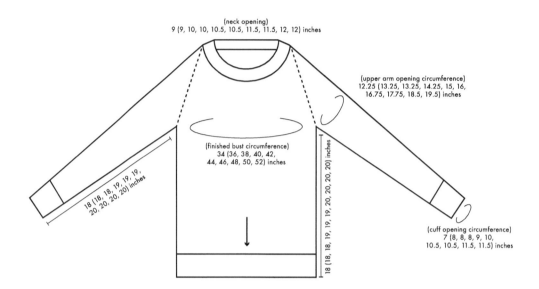

(neck opening)
9 (9, 10, 10, 10.5, 10.5, 11.5, 11.5, 12, 12) inches

(upper arm opening circumference)
12.25 (13.25, 13.25, 14.25, 15, 16, 16.75, 17.75, 18.5, 19.5) inches

(finished bust circumference)
34 (36, 38, 40, 42, 44, 46, 48, 50, 52) inches

18 (18, 18, 19, 19, 19, 20, 20, 20, 20) inches

18 (18, 18, 19, 19, 20, 20, 20, 20) inches

(cuff opening circumference)
7 (8, 8, 8, 9, 10, 10.5, 10.5, 11.5, 11.5) inches

Sleeves
Starting at underarm and using larger needles, transfer one set of reserved sleeve stitches from holder to needles and pick up 4 CO underarm sts. PM to mark beginning of rnd. 29 (31, 31, 33, 35, 36, 38, 40, 42, 44) sts rem.

Join new end of working yarn (leaving a tail for finishing), pm and begin working in Stockinette Stitch.

Decrease Rnd: K to end of rnd, ssk, sl m, ktog to decrease 1 st on each side of marker every 6 rnds, 6 (6, 6, 7, 7, 7, 7, 8, 8, 9) times. 17 (19, 19, 19, 21, 22, 24, 24, 26, 26) sts rem.

Continue working in Stockinette Stitch until sleeve measures 18 (18, 18, 19, 19, 19, 20, 20, 20, 20) inches from underarm.

Note: For all sizes with an odd stitch count, k2tog last two sts of final stockinette round before starting cuff.

Cuff
Next Rnd: Work in 1x1 rib (k1, p1) for 7 rnds.

BO in pattern, loosely. Break yarn.

Repeat for remaining sleeve.

Neck
Working in the round and starting at the left back raglan, pick up and k 20 (20, 22, 22, 24, 24, 26, 26, 28, 28) sts evenly around neck using smaller needles.

Next Rnd: Work in 1x1 rib (k1, p1) for 4 rnds.
BO in pattern, loosely. Break yarn.

FINISHING
Use tapestry needle and yarn tail at underarm to close and neaten gap under each arm. Weave in all ends.

BLOCKING
Follow dye instructions first if desired. Soak garment in bowl of lukewarm water and a few drops of no-rinse fabric wash. Gently wring out and lay garment on a towel and use towel to remove excess water. Lay out garment and shape to desired shape and dimensions. Allow to dry completely.

Hunter

DESIGN NOTES
Hunter is a unisex linen stitch cowl with fantastic texture worked seamlessly in the round. The sample shown in this book was left unaltered but this cowl would look great dip-dyed or painted.

SIZES
One size

FINISHED MEASUREMENTS
30 inch circumference and 11 inches from top to bottom

YARN
Wool and the Gang Crazy Sexy Wool in Eagle Grey (Super Bulky, 100% Peruvian wool; 87 yards per 200 g ball) 1 ball (87 yards)

NEEDLES
US 19 (16 mm) 16" circular needles (or size needed to obtain gauge)

NOTIONS
Stitch marker
Tapestry needle

GAUGE
4 inches = 6 sts and 13 rows in Linen Stitch on size 19 (16 mm) needles, unblocked

STITCH GUIDE
Linen Stitch (worked in the round)
Rnd 1: K1, *sl 1 wyif, k1; rep from * to end of rnd.
Rnd 2: Sl 1 wyif, *k1, sl 1 wyif; rep from * to end of rnd.
Rep rows 1 and 2 for pattern.

Garter Stitch (worked in the round)
Rnd 1: P all sts.
Rnd 2: K all sts.
Rnd 3: P all sts.

ABBREVIATIONS
CO - cast on
BO - bind off
k – knit
st(s) - stitch(es)
rnd - round
p - purl
pm - place marker
rep - repeat
rnd(s) - round(s)
sl - slip
wyif - with yarn in front

DIRECTIONS
Using long-tail method on US 19 needles, CO 43 sts. Join to work in the round, taking care not to twist sts. PM to mark beginning of round.

Work Rnds 1-3 of Garter Stitch once.

Next rnd: Work in Linen Stitch until piece measures 10 inches from CO edge.

Work Rnds 1-2 of Garter Stitch once.

BO all sts purlwise, loosely.

FINISHING
Cut yarn, leaving a 6-8 inch tail. Using tapestry needle, weave in ends.

BLOCKING
I do not recommend blocking this particular yarn/garment. If blocking is needed, lay out garment and shape to desired shape and dimensions. Gently spritz with water in a spray bottle until damp, but not soaking wet. Allow to dry completely.

Halo

DESIGN NOTES

Halo is a wrap made of an extra long cowl that is stitched to make sleeve openings. The sample shown here was splattered with black fabric paint. Find detailed paint instructions in the 'Dye, Bleach and Paint Techniques' section on page 130.

SIZES
XS, S, M, L, XL

FINISHED MEASUREMENTS (after blocking)
60 (64, 68, 72, 76 inch circumference and 15 inches from top to bottom

YARN
Color A: Shibui Rain in Tar (DK, 100% Cotton; 135 yards per 50 g skein)
1 skein (135 yards)

Color B: Shibui Lunar in Tar (Lace, 60% Extra Fine Merino, 40% Mulberry Silk; 401 yards per 50 g skein)
1 skein (401 yards)

Color C: Shibui Reed in Tar (Fingering, 100% Linen; 246 yards per 50 g skein)
1 skein (246 yards)

Color D: Shibui Staccato in Tar (Fingering, 70% Superwash Merino, 30% Silk; 191 yards per 50 g skein)
1 skein (191 yards)

Color E: Shibui Cima in Tar (Lace, 70% Superbaby Alpaca, 30% Fine Merino; 328 yards per 50 g skein)
1 skein (328 yards)

Color F: Shibui Birch in Tar (Sport, 100% Extra Fine Merino; 262 yards per 50 g skein)
1 skein (262 yards)

NEEDLES
US 7 (4.5 mm) 24" circular needles
(or size needed to obtain gauge)

NOTIONS
2 locking stitch markers
Measuring tape
Tapestry needle

GAUGE
4 inches = 20 sts and 30 rows in Stockinette Stitch with yarn held double on size US 7 (4.5 mm) needles

STITCH GUIDE
Single Rib
All rnds: *K1, p1, rep from * to end of rnd.

Stockinette Stitch
All rnds: K all sts.

ABBREVIATIONS
approx. - approximately
CO - cast on
BO - bind off
k – knit
st(s) - stitch(es)
rnd(s) - round(s)
p - purl
patt - pattern
pm - place marker

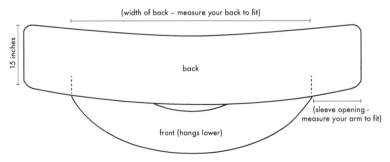

Total circumference after blocking: 60 (64, 68, 72, 76 inches

DIRECTIONS

With Colors A and B held together and using long-tail method on US 7 needles, CO 260 (280, 300, 320, 340) sts. Join to work in the round, taking care not to twist sts. PM to mark beginning of round.

Work Single Rib stitch pattern for 4 rnds total.

Begin working in Stockinette Stitch until piece measures approx. 5 inches from CO edge (or until yarn runs out.)

Break yarn, and with Colors C and D held together, continue working in Stockinette Stitch until piece measures approx. 10 inches from CO edge (or until yarn runs out.)

Break yarn, and with Colors E and F held together, continue working in Stockinette Stitch until piece measures approx. 14½ inches from CO edge.

With Colors E and F held together, work Single Rib stitch patt for 3 rnds total.

BO all sts in pattern, loosely.

FINISHING

Cut yarn, leaving a 6-8 inch tail. Using tapestry needle, weave in all ends.

To make arm openings, use measuring tape to measure the width of your back from underarm to underarm. Use 2 locking stitch markers to mark that length plus 2 inches along the bottom edge of piece. Use measuring tape to measure the circumference of your upper arm. Starting with the marker on the right side of your back measurements, create an opening using your arm circumference measurement. Pinch the fabric into a 'sleeve' and attach that fabric to the marker on the right side. Do the same for the left side. Using leftover yarn, Make a seam 1½ inches long vertically at each marker. When worn, this cowl/wrap will lay flat across your back and the cowl will hang loosely in the front. See schematic.

BLOCKING

Soak garment in bowl of lukewarm water and a few drops of no-rinse fabric wash. Gently squeeze water out and lay garment on a towel and use towel to remove excess water. Lay out garment and shape to desired shape and dimensions. Allow to dry completely.

Twig

DESIGN NOTES
Twig is a fun reversible hat with an off-set rib. The hat shown was left unaltered but take your finished project one step further using the techniques explained in the 'Dye, Bleach and Paint Techniques' section on page 130 of this book.

SIZES
One size

FINISHED MEASUREMENTS
20-inch circumference

YARN
Third Piece Funky Chunky in Citrine (Super Bulky, 100% merino wool; 82 yards per 200 g ball)
1 ball (82 yards)

NEEDLES
US 15 (12 mm) 16" circular needles (or size needed to obtain gauge)
US 15 (12 mm) DPNs

NOTIONS
Stitch marker
Tapestry needle

GAUGE
4 inches = 7 sts and 10 rows in Stockinette Stitch on US 15 (10 mm) needles

STITCH GUIDE
Single Rib (worked in the round)
All rnds: *P1, k1, rep from *.

Stockinette Stitch (worked in the round)
All rnds: K all sts.

ABBREVIATIONS
CO - cast on
k - knit
k2tog - knit 2 sts together
p - purl
pm - place marker
rem - remaining
rep - repeat
rnd(s) - round(s)
st(s) - stitch(es)
st st - stockinette stitch

DIRECTIONS
Using long-tail method and US 17 circular needle, CO 32 sts. Join for working in the round and PM, taking care not to twist sts.

Work Single Rib stitch pattern for 4 rnds total.

Next rnd: Work 16 sts in Single Rib stitch pattern, k to end of rnd. Repeat for 4 more rnds.

Next rnd: Work in Stockinette Stitch until piece measures 7 inches from CO edge.

SHAPE CROWN
Switching to Stockinette Stitch pattern, shape crown as follows, changing to DPNs when necessary.

Decrease Rnd 1: *K 6 sts, k2tog, rep from * to end of rnd. 28 sts rem (4 sts decreased).

Next Rnd: K all sts.

Decrease Rnd 2: *K 5 sts, k2tog, rep from * to end of rnd. 24 sts rem (4 sts decreased).

Next Rnd: K all sts.

Decrease Rnd 3: *K 4 sts, k2tog, rep from * to end of rnd. 20 sts rem (4 sts decreased).

Next Rnd: K all sts.

Decrease Rnd 4: *K 3 sts, k2tog, rep from * to end of rnd. 16 sts rem (4 sts decreased).

Next Rnd: K all sts.

Decrease Rnd 5: *K 2 sts, k2tog, rep from * to end of rnd. 12 sts rem (4 sts decreased).

Next Rnd: K all sts.

Decrease Rnd 6: *K2tog, rep from * to end of rnd. 6 sts rem (6 sts decreased).

FINISHING
Cut yarn, leaving a 6-8 in tail. Using tapestry needle, thread rem sts onto tail. Pull tight and secure, weave in ends. Turn inside-out to wear as shown (reverse stockinette) or leave as-is with the stockinette side facing out.

BLOCKING
I do not recommend blocking this particular yarn/garment. If blocking is needed, lay out garment and shape to desired shape and dimensions. Gently spritz with water in a spray bottle until damp, but not soaking wet. Allow to dry completely.

Echo

DESIGN NOTES

This seed stitch cowl with garter stitch edging is my go-to accessory and is a super quick knit that you can whip up in no time. The cowl shown here was splattered with black fabric paint. See 'Dye, Bleach and Paint Techniques' section on page 130 for more info.

SIZES

One size

FINISHED MEASUREMENTS

30 inch circumference and 10 inches from top to bottom

YARN

Third Piece Funky Chunky in Cloud (Super Bulky, 100% merino wool; 82 yards per 200 g ball)
1 ball (82 yards)

NEEDLES

US 19 (16 mm) 24 inch circular needles
(or size needed to obtain gauge)

NOTIONS

Stitch marker
Tapestry needle

GAUGE

4 inches = 5 sts and 9 rows in Seed Stitch on size US 19 (16 mm) needles, unblocked

STITCH GUIDE

Seed Stitch (worked in the round)
Rnd 1: *k1, p1, rep from * to last st of rnd, k1.
Rnd 2: p1, *k1, p1, rep from * to end of rnd.
Rep rnds 1 and 2 for pattern.

Garter Stitch
Rnd 1: P all sts.
Rnd 2: K all sts.
Rnd 3: P all sts.

ABBREVIATIONS

CO - cast on
BO - bind off
k – knit
st(s) - stitch(es)
rnd(s) - round(s)
p - purl
pm - place marker
rep - repeat

DIRECTIONS

Using long-tail method on US 19 needles, CO 39 sts. Join to work in the round, taking care not to twist sts. PM to mark beginning of round.

Work rnds 1-3 of Garter Stitch.

Next rnd: Work in Seed Stitch until piece measures 9 inches from CO edge.

Work rnds 1 & 2 of Garter Stitch.

BO all sts purlwise, loosely.

FINISHING

Cut yarn, leaving a 6-8 inch tail. Using tapestry needle, weave in ends.

BLOCKING

I do not recommend blocking this particular yarn/garment. If blocking is needed, lay out garment and shape to desired shape and dimensions. Gently spritz with water in a spray bottle until damp, but not soaking wet. Allow to dry completely.

Space

DESIGN NOTES
Worked seamlessly in the round, this cowl is unisex and reversible. Wear it with the stockinette side facing out or turn it inside-out to see the bold reverse stockinette stitch stripes.

SIZES
One size

FINISHED MEASUREMENTS
24 inch circumference and 16 inches from top to bottom

YARN
Color A: Madelinetosh ASAP in Onyx (Super Bulky, 100% Merino wool; 90 yards per 127 g ball)
1 ball (90 yards)

Color B Madelinetosh ASAP in 'Optic' (Super Bulky, 100% Merino wool; 90 yards per 127 g ball)
1 ball (90 yards)

NEEDLES
US 11 (8 mm) 24" circular needles
(or size needed to obtain gauge)

NOTIONS
Tapestry needle
Stitch Marker

GAUGE
4 inches = 10 sts and 15 rows in St st on size 11 (8 mm) needles, unblocked

STITCH GUIDE
Stockinette Stitch
All rnds: K all sts.

Garter Stitch
Rnd 1: P all sts.
Rnd 2: K all sts.
Rnd 3: P all sts.

ABBREVIATIONS
CO - cast on
BO - bind off
k – knit
st(s) - stitch(es)
rnd(s) - round(s)
pm - place marker
st st - stockinette stitch

DIRECTIONS
Using long-tail method on US 11 needles, CO 63 sts. Join to work in the round, taking care not to twist sts. PM to mark beginning of round.

Begin working with Color A:
Rnd 1: P all sts.
Rnd 2: K all sts.
Rnd 3: P all sts.

Join Color B and begin working in stockinette stitch:
Rnd 4: K all sts with Color B.
Rnd 5: K all sts with Color A.

Repeat rnds 4 & 5 until piece measures 15 1/2 inches from CO edge, then knit rnd 4 one more time.

Cut Color B. With Color A, work rnds 1-3 once.

BO all sts purlwise, loosely.

FINISHING
Cut yarn, leaving a 6-8 inch tail. Using tapestry needle, weave in ends.

BLOCKING
I do not recommend blocking this particular yarn/garment. If blocking is needed, lay out garment and shape to desired shape and dimensions. Gently spritz with water in a spray bottle until damp, but not soaking wet. Allow to dry completely.

Link

DESIGN NOTES
Link is a cowl for everyone. This unisex cowl is knit in the round and is the perfect throw-on accessory (in such a fun color.) The sample shown was left unaltered but take your finished hat one step further using the techniques explained in the 'Dye, Bleach and Paint Techniques' section on page 130.

SIZES
One size

FINISHED MEASUREMENTS
33 inch circumference and 9 inches from top to bottom

YARN
Third Piece Funky Chunky in Citrine (Super Bulky, 100% merino wool; 82 yards per 200 g ball)
1 ball (82 yards)

NEEDLES
US 19 (16 mm) 24 inch circular needles
(or size needed to obtain gauge)

NOTIONS
Tapestry needle
Stitch marker

GAUGE
4 inches = 5 sts and 6 rows in Garter Stitch on size 19 (16 mm) needles, unblocked

STITCH GUIDE
Garter Stitch (worked in the round)
Rnd 1: P all sts.
Rnd 2: K all sts.
Rep rnds 1 and 2 for pattern.

ABBREVIATIONS
CO - cast on
BO - bind off
k – knit
st(s) - stitch(es)
rnd(s) - round(s)
p - purl
pm - place marker
rep - repeat

DIRECTIONS
Using long-tail method on US 19 needles, CO 43 sts. Join to work in the round, taking care not to twist sts. PM to mark beginning of round.

Work in Garter Stitch until piece measures 9 inches from CO edge.

BO all sts, loosely.

FINISHING
Cut yarn, leaving a 6-8 inch tail. Using tapestry needle, weave in ends.

BLOCKING
I do not recommend blocking this particular yarn/garment. If blocking is needed, lay out garment and shape to desired shape and dimensions. Gently spritz with water in a spray bottle until damp, but not soaking wet. Allow to dry completely.

Ash

DESIGN NOTES

Ash is a unisex top-down cable raglan, worked seamless in the round. This sweater was dip-dyed after knitting using the techniques explained in the 'Dye, Bleach and Paint Techniques' section on page 130. Read all directions before knitting – some steps are worked simultaneously/at the same time.

SIZES

34 (36, 38, 40, 42, 44, 46)

To Fit Bust: 34 (36, 38, 40, 42, 44, 46) inches with 2 inches ease

FINISHED MEASUREMENTS (after blocking)

36 (38, 40, 42, 44, 46, 48) inches

YARN

Wool and the Gang Heal the Wool in Rocky Grey (Super bulky; 100% recycled Peruvian wool fiber; 87 yards per 200g ball)
5 (6, 6, 7, 7, 8, 9) balls
435 (522, 522, 609, 609, 696, 783) yards

NEEDLES

US 17 (12 mm) 36" circular needles (or size needed to obtain gauge)
US 17 (12 mm) 8 in double pointed needles (or size needed to obtain gauge)

NOTIONS

Cable needle
Stitch markers (5)
Stitch holders or scrap yarn
Tapestry needle

GAUGE

4 inches = 6 sts and 9 rnds in St st on US 17 needles

STITCH GUIDE

Stockinette Stitch (in the round)
K all sts.

Single Rib (in the round):
All rnds: *K1, p1, rep from *.

Woven Cable (worked in the rnd over center front 18 sts)
Rnds 1 & 2: K 18 sts.
Rnd 3: (C6B) 3 times.
Rnds 4-6: K 18 sts.
Rnd 7: K3 (C6F) 2 times, k3.
Rnd 8: K 18 sts.

ABBREVIATIONS

CO - cast on
BO - bind off
beg - beginning
C6B - slip 3 stitches purlwise onto cable needle, at back of work. Work 3 stitches. Slide 3 cable stitches over and knit.
C6F - slip 3 stitches purlwise to front of work. Work stitches on needle, then work stitches on cable needle.
k – knit
k2tog - knit 2 sts together (1 st decreased)
inc – increase
m - marker
m1r – make one right (pick up the bar between the stitch you've knitted and the one you're about to knit from back to front, knit through the front of new loop)
m1l – make one left (pick up the bar between the stitch you've knitted and the one you're about to knit from front to back, knit through the back of new loop)
p - purl
pm - place marker
rep - repeat
rem - remain(ing)
rnd(s) - round(s)
RS - right side
st(s) - stitch(es)
sl – slip
ssk - slip, slip, knit these two stitches together (1 st decreased)
WS - wrong side

DIRECTIONS

Using long-tail method and US 17 needles, CO 18 (18, 20, 20, 22, 22, 24) sts. Do not join; work flat.

Set-up Row (WS): P1, pm, p3 (3, 3, 3, 3, 3, 3) sts, pm, p 10 (10, 12, 12, 14, 14, 16) sts, pm, p3 (3, 3, 3, 3, 3, 3) sts, pm; p1.

Raglan Increases

Next Row (RS inc): K1, m1r, knit to first marker, sl m, *k1, m1l, k to 1 st before marker, m1r, k1, sl m; repeat from * 2 more times, k to 1 st before end of row; m1l, k1. 8 sts increased. 26 (26, 28, 28, 30, 30, 32) sts.

Next Row (WS): P across.

Repeat these 2 rnds 9 (10, 11, 11, 11, 12, 12) more times.

AT THE SAME TIME: After working first 4 rows, CO 1 st at each end of needle for neck edge. (2 sts increased)

Next Row: CO 2 sts at each end of needle. (4 sts increased)

Next RS Row: CO 4 (4, 4, 4, 4, 4, 4) sts at center front. Join in round, taking care not to twist sts.

108 (116, 130, 126, 128, 136, 138) sts rem.

AT THE SAME TIME: After working first 4 rows after joining in the rnd, place stitch markers on each side of front center 18 sts for cable panel. Work in Stockinette Stitch and Woven Cable (on 18 sts between markers) as you work increase rounds.

Divide for body and sleeves

32 (34, 36, 36, 36, 38, 38) front sts; 23 (25, 27, 27, 27, 29, 29) right sleeve sts; 30 (32, 36, 36, 38, 40, 42) back sts; 23 (25, 27, 27, 27, 29, 29) left sleeve sts.

Work 30 (32, 36, 36, 38, 40, 42) sts for back, then place next 23 (25, 27, 27, 27, 29, 29) sts on holder for right sleeve; CO 4 sts, work 32 (34, 36, 36, 36, 38, 38) sts (front), place next 23 (25, 27, 27, 27, 29, 29) sts on holder for left sleeve; CO 4 sts.

70 (74, 80, 80, 82, 86, 88) sts rem for body.

Work body in Stockinette Stitch and Woven Cable until piece measures 16 (17, 17, 18, 18, 19, 19) inches from underarm.

Work in Single Rib (in the rnd) for 6 rnds.

BO all sts.

Sleeves

Starting at underarm and using larger needles, transfer one set of reserved sleeve stitches from holder to needles and pick up 4 CO underarm sts. PM to mark beginning of rnd. 27 (29, 31, 31, 31, 33, 33) sts.

Join new end of working yarn (leaving a tail for finishing), pm and begin working in Stockinette Stitch.

Decrease Rnd: K to end of rnd, ssk, sl m, ktog to decrease 1 st on each side of marker every 6 rnds, 6 (6, 7, 7, 6, 7, 6) times. 15 (17, 17, 17, 19, 19, 21) sts rem.

Continue until sleeve measures 16 (17, 17, 18, 18, 19, 19) inches from underarm.

Note: For all sizes, k2tog last two sts of final stockinette round before starting cuff.

Cuff

Next Rnd: Work Single Rib (in the rnd) for 6 rnds.
BO in pattern, loosely. Break yarn.

Repeat for remaining sleeve.

Neck

Working in the round and starting at the left back raglan, pick up and k 20 sts evenly around neck using smaller needles (you can pick up more sts for if you prefer a wider neck opening; see schematic for finished neck measurement as written).

Next Rnd: Work in Single Rib (in the rnd) for 3 rnds.
BO in pattern, loosely. Break yarn.

FINISHING

Use tapestry needle and yarn tail at underarm to close and neaten gap under each arm. Weave in all ends.

BLOCKING

Follow dye instructions first if desired. Soak garment in bowl of lukewarm water and a few drops of no-rinse fabric wash. Gently wring out and lay garment on a towel and use towel to remove excess water. Lay out garment and shape to desired shape and dimensions. Allow to dry completely.

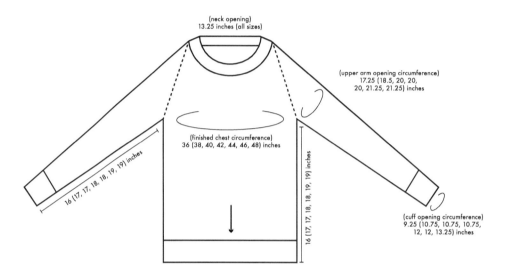

(neck opening)
13.25 inches (all sizes)

(upper arm opening circumference)
17.25 (18.5, 20, 20,
20, 21.25, 21.25) inches

(finished chest circumference)
36 (38, 40, 42, 44, 46, 48) inches

16 (17, 17, 18, 18, 19, 19) inches

16 (17, 17, 18, 18, 19, 19) inches

(cuff opening circumference)
9.25 (10.75, 10.75, 10.75,
12, 12, 13.25) inches

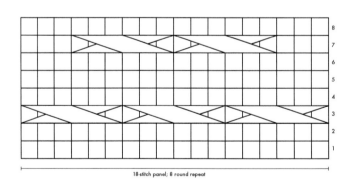

8
7
6
5
4
3
2
1

18-stitch panel; 8 round repeat

Cloud

DESIGN NOTES

Cloud is a unisex must-have, must-knit super scarf. The sample shown was left unaltered but take your finished scarf one step further using the techniques explained in the 'Dye, Bleach and Paint Techniques' section at the back of this book.

SIZES

One size

FINISHED MEASUREMENTS

6 inches wide and 105 inches long

YARN

Third Piece Funky Chunky in Steel (Super Bulky, 100% merino wool; 82 yards per 200 g ball)
2 balls (164 yards)

NEEDLES

US 19 (16 mm) needles
(or size needed to obtain gauge)

NOTIONS

Tapestry needle

GAUGE

4 inches = 6 sts and 13 rows in Garter Stitch on size 19 (16 mm) needles, unblocked

STITCH GUIDE

Garter Stitch
Row 1 (RS): K all sts.
Row 2 (WS): K all sts.

2x2 Rib:
Row 1 (RS): *K2, p2, rep from * to end of row.
Row 2 (WS): *P2, k2, rep from * to end of row.

ABBREVIATIONS

CO - cast on

BO - bind off

k – knit

st(s) - stitch(es)

p - purl

pm - place marker

rep - repeat

DIRECTIONS

Using long-tail method on US 19 needles, CO 10 sts.

Work in 2x2 Rib stitch for 12 rows total.

Garter section: PM to mark RS; work in Garter Stitch for 6 inches, ending with RS row.

Stockinette Break 1:
Row 1 (WS): K2, p5, k3.
Row 2 (RS): K all sts.

Garter section: PM to mark RS; work in Garter Stitch for 6 inches, ending with RS row.

Stockinette Break 2:
Row 1 (WS): K4, p4, k2.
Row 2 (RS): K all sts.

Repeat Garter sections and Stockinette breaks until piece measures 99 in from CO edge.

Work in 2x2 Rib stitch for 11 rows total.

BO all sts in pattern, loosely.

FINISHING

Cut yarn, leaving a 6-8 inch tail. Using tapestry needle, weave in ends.

BLOCKING

I do not recommend blocking this particular yarn/garment. If blocking is needed, lay out garment and shape to desired shape and dimensions. Gently spritz with water in a spray bottle until damp, but not soaking wet. Allow to dry completely.

California

DESIGN NOTES

California is a super speedy unisex super bulky hat that will fit almost anyone. This hat is seamless and worked in the round. I left the samples in this book unaltered but California would look great dip-dyed or splattered with fabric paint.

SIZES

One size

FINISHED MEASUREMENTS

19 inch circumference (unstretched)

YARN

Wool and the Gang Crazy Sexy Wool in Tweed Grey or 'Sand Trooper Beige' (Super Bulky, 100% Peruvian wool; 87 yards per 200 g ball)
1 ball (87 yards)

NEEDLES

US 19 (16 mm) 16" circular needles (or size needed to obtain gauge)
US 19 (16 mm) DPNs

NOTIONS

Stitch marker
Tapestry needle

GAUGE

4 inches = 5 1/2 sts and 9 rows in Stockinette Stitch on US 19 (16 mm) needles

STITCH GUIDE

Single Rib (worked in the round)
All rnds: *P1, k1, rep from *.

Stockinette Stitch (worked in the round)
All rnds: K all sts.

ABBREVIATIONS

CO - cast on

k - knit

k2tog - knit 2 stitches together

p - purl

pm - place marker

rep - repeat

rnd(s) - round(s)

st(s) - stitch(es)

DIRECTIONS

Using long-tail method and US 19 circular needle, CO 24 sts. Join for working in the round and PM, taking care not to twist sts.

Work Single Rib stitch pattern for 7 rnds total.

Work in Stockinette Stitch until piece measures 7 inches from CO edge.

SHAPE CROWN

Shape crown as follows, switching to DPNs when necessary.

Decrease Rnd 1: *K4, k2tog. Rep from * to end of rnd. 20 sts rem (4 sts decreased).

Next rnd: K all sts.

Decrease Rnd 2: *K3, k2tog. Rep from * to end of rnd. 16 sts rem (4 sts decreased).

Next rnd: K all sts.

Decrease Rnd 3: *K2, k2tog. Rep from * to end of rnd. 12 sts rem (4 sts decreased).

Next rnd: K all sts.

Decrease Rnd 4: *K2tog, rep from * to end of rnd. 6 sts rem. (6 sts decreased).

FINISHING

Cut yarn, leaving a 6-8 in tail. Using tapestry needle, thread rem sts onto tail. Pull tight and secure, weave in ends.

BLOCKING

I do not recommend blocking this particular yarn/garment. If blocking is needed, lay out garment and shape to desired shape and dimensions. Gently spritz with water in a spray bottle until damp, but not soaking wet. Allow to dry completely.

Venice

DESIGN NOTES

Venice is a simple unisex hat that becomes anything but basic once you add bleach. I highly recommend using the yarn suggested below (Rowan Denim) because it's the only yarn I've found that bleaches to pure white. Find detailed bleach instructions in the 'Dye, Bleach and Paint Techniques' section on page 130 of this book.

SIZES

One size

FINISHED MEASUREMENTS

(after blocking, unstretched)
9 inches tall and 20 inch circumference

YARN

Rowan Denim in Black (DK; 100% Cotton; 98 yds per 50 g ball)
2 balls
196 yards

NEEDLES

US 6 (4 mm) 16 inch circular needles
(or size needed to obtain gauge)

NOTIONS

Tapestry needle
Stitch Marker

GAUGE

4 inches = 17 sts and 32 rows in Stockinette Stitch on US 6 (4 mm) needles

STITCH GUIDE

Single Rib (worked in the round)
All rnds: *P1, k1, rep from * to end of rnd.

Stockinette Stitch (worked in the round)
All rnds: K all sts.

ABBREVIATIONS

CO - cast on
DPN(s) - double pointed needle(s)
k – knit
k2tog - knit 2 stitches together
st(s) - stitch(es)
p - purl
pm - place marker
rem - remain
rep - repeat
rnd(s) - round(s)

DIRECTIONS

Using long-tail method and US 6 (4 mm) needles, CO 90 sts. Join for working in the round and PM, taking care not to twist sts.

Work Single Rib stitch pattern for 16 rnds total.

Begin working Stockinette Stitch in the rnd until piece measures 7 inches from CO edge.

CROWN SHAPING (Switch to DPNs when necessary)

Decrease Rnd 1: *K 7 sts, k2tog, rep from * to end of rnd. 80 sts rem (10 sts decreased).

Next Rnd: K all sts.

Decrease Rnd 2: *K 6 sts, k2tog, rep from * to end of rnd. 70 sts rem (10 sts decreased).

Next Rnd: K all sts.

Decrease Rnd 3: *K 5 sts, k2tog, rep from * to end of rnd. 60 sts rem (10 sts decreased).

Next Rnd: K all sts.

Decrease Rnd 4: *K 4 sts, k2tog, rep from * to end of rnd. 50 sts rem (10 sts decreased).

Next Rnd: K all sts.

Decrease Rnd 5: *K 3 sts, k2tog, rep from * to end of rnd. 40 sts rem (10 sts decreased).

Next Rnd: K all sts.

Decrease Rnd 6: *K 2 sts, k2tog, rep from * to end of rnd. 30 sts rem (10 sts decreased).

Next Rnd: K all sts.

Decrease Rnd 7: *K2tog, rep from * to end of rnd. 15 sts rem (15 sts decreased).

FINISHING

Cut yarn, leaving a 6-8 inch tail. Using tapestry needle, weave in ends.

BLEACHING (optional)

If you choose to bleach your hat, do so before blocking. Cover your work area to protect surface underneath (or work outdoors.) Use a paintbrush to splatter bleach onto hat, or drip small amounts using a small container or the cap of the bleach bottle. Find detailed bleach tips on page 130 of this book.

BLOCKING

Soak hat in bowl of lukewarm water and a few drops of no-rinse fabric wash. Gently wring out and lay garment on a towel and use towel to remove excess water. Lay out garment and shape to desired shape and dimensions. Allow to dry completely.

Rebel

DESIGN NOTES

Rebel is a unisex basic tank with a knit side and a purl side that is worked seamless in the round from the bottom up, then worked flat and seamed at the shoulders. Fabric paint was used on the samples shown to create hand-painted lettering and a splattered effect. Find detailed paint instructions in the 'Dye, Bleach and Paint Techniques' section on page 130.

SIZES

To Fit Bust: 34 (38, 42, 46, 50, 54) inches

FINISHED MEASUREMENTS

34.5 (38.5, 42.5, 46.5, 50.5, 54.5) inches

YARN

Wool and the Gang Crazy Sexy Wool in Space Black
(Super Bulky, 100% Peruvian wool; 87 yards per 200 g ball)
3 (3, 4, 4, 5, 5) balls
261 (261, 348, 348, 435, 435) yards

NEEDLES

US 19 (15 mm) 29" circular needles (or size needed to obtain gauge)

NOTIONS

Stitch marker
Tapestry needle

GAUGE

4 inches = 8 sts and 12 rows in St st on size 15 (10 mm) needles, unblocked

STITCH GUIDE

Stockinette Stitch (in the round)
K all sts.

Stockinette Stitch (flat):
Row 1 (RS): Sl 1, k all sts.
Row 2 (WS): Sl 1, p all sts.

Reverse Stockinette Stitch (in the round)
P all sts.

Reverse Stockinette Stitch (flat):
Row 1 (RS): Sl 1, P all sts.
Row 2 (WS): Sl 1, K all sts.

Single Rib Stitch (in the round);
All rnds: *K1, p1, rep from *.

ABBREVIATIONS

beg - beginning

BO - bind off

CO - cast on

cont - continue

k – knit

k2tog - knit 2 stitches together (1 st decreased)

p - purl

p2tog - purl 2 stitches together (1 st decreased)

pm - place marker

rep - repeat

rem - remain

rnd(s) - round(s)

RS - right side

sl – slip

st(s) - stitch(es)

WS - wrong side

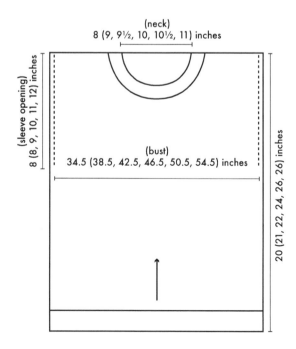

(neck)
8 (9, 9½, 10, 10½, 11) inches

(sleeve opening)
8 (8, 9, 10, 11, 12) inches

(bust)
34.5 (38.5, 42.5, 46.5, 50.5, 54.5) inches

20 (21, 22, 24, 26, 26) inches

DIRECTIONS

Using long-tail method and US 19 (16 mm) needles, CO 52 (58, 64, 70, 76, 82) sts. Join to work in the round, taking care not to twist sts. PM to mark beginning of round.

Work in Single Rib Stitch for 4 rnds total.

Begin working Stockinette Stitch (in the rnd) for 26 (29, 32, 35, 38, 41) sts and then Reverse Stockinette Stitch for 26 (29, 32, 35, 38, 41) sts until piece measures 12 (13, 13, 14, 15, 15) inches from CO edge.

Transfer last 26 (29, 32, 35, 38, 41) sts of rnd to stitch holders or scrap yarn to be worked for Front. 26 (29, 32, 35, 38, 41) sts rem on needles for Back.

BACK (work flat)
Next row (RS): P 26 (29, 32, 35, 38, 41) sts.

Next row (WS): Turn work and, slipping first st, k to end of row.

Slipping first st of every row, cont working in Reverse Stockinette Stitch until arm opening measures 8 (8, 9, 10, 11, 12) inches.

At beg of next 2 rows, BO 5 (5, 6, 7, 7, 8) sts. 16 (19, 20, 21, 24, 25) sts rem.

BO rem sts for back of neck.

FRONT (work flat)
Transfer held 26 (29, 32, 35, 38, 41) sts to needles and work in Stockinette Stitch as for back until arm openings measure 6 (7, 8, 9, 9.5, 9.5) inches, ending with WS row.

With RS facing, k 8 (10, 10, 12, 12, 13) sts.

Join new yarn and BO center 10 (9, 12, 11, 14, 15) for crew neck.

K 8 (10, 10, 12, 12, 13) sts to end of row.

8 (10, 10, 12, 12, 13) sts rem on each side.

Work each side at the same time using separate balls of yarn:

Next row (WS): P to last 2 sts, p2tog across first set of sts; P2tog, p to end across second set of sts. 7 (9, 9, 11, 11, 12) sts rem each side.

Next row (RS): K to last 2 sts, k2tog across first set of sts; K2tog, k to end across second set of sts. 6 (8, 8, 10, 10, 11) sts rem each side.

Purl across both sets of sts.

Next row (RS): K to last 2 sts, k2tog across first set of sts; K2tog, k to end across second set of sts 1 (1, 1, 2, 2, 2) more times. 5 (7, 7, 8, 8, 9) sts rem on each side.

Work even until shoulders on front measure the same as the back.

BO rem sts.

SEAMING
Seam shoulder using shoulder seam stitch, or sew a simple seam with the edges exposed.

NECK
With smaller needles, right side facing and starting at right shoulder, pick up and knit 30 (32, 36, 40, 44) sts around neck opening.
Next rnd: Work Single Rib Stitch (in the round) for 3 rnds total. BO in pattern, loosely.

FINISHING
Using tapestry needle, weave in ends.

BLOCKING
I do not recommend blocking this particular yarn/garment. If blocking is needed, lay out garment and shape to desired shape and dimensions. Gently spritz with water in a spray bottle until damp, but not soaking wet. Allow to dry completely.

RESOURCES

YARN

Ewe Ewe Yarns
www.eweewe.com

Knit Safari
www.knitsafari.com

Loopy Mango
www.loopymango.com

Madelinetosh
www.madelinetosh.com

Rowan Yarns
www.knitrowan.com

Shibui
www.shibuiknits.com

Spud & Chloë by Blue Sky Fibers
www.spudandchloe.com

Third Piece
www.thirdpiece.com

Wool and the Gang
www.woolandthegang.com

NEEDLES & SUPPLIES

Field Notes
www.fieldnotesbrand.com

Fringe Supply Co.
www.fringesupplyco.com

**Knitter's Pride Cubics
Interchangeable Needles**
www.knitterspride.com

Loopy Mango
(size 36 and 50 circular needles)
www.loopymango.com

**Lykke Driftwood
Interchangeable Needles**
www.lykkecrafts.com/

Rit Dye
www.ritdye.com

Tulip Fabric Paint
(Fabric Spray Paint and Color
Shot Fabric Paint)
www.ilovetocreate.com

ABBREVIATIONS

beg	beginning
BO	bind off
CO	cast on
cont	continue
dec	decrease
DPN	double pointed needle
est	established
foll	following
in	inches
inc	increase
k	knit
k2tog	knit 2 together (1 stitch decreased)
kf&b	knit into front and back of stitch (one stitch increased)
ktbl	knit through back loop
kw	knitwise
mm	millimeters
m1r	make one right
m1l	make one left
p	purl
p2tog	purl 2 sts together (1 stitch decreased)
patt	pattern
pm	place marker
pu	pick up
rem	remaining
rep	repeat
rnd(s)	round(s)
RS	right side
sl	slip
sm	slip marker
ssk	slip slip knit (1 stitch decreased)
st(s)	stitch(es)
st st	stockinette stitch
tog	together
WS	wrong side
yo	yarn over

DYE, BLEACH AND PAINT TECHNIQUES

Now it's time for the fun part. In this section I will share some of the tips and techniques I learned as I created the garments in this book. There are a million other ways to alter your knits than what I've listed below, so be open to your own ideas. Explore and experiment, test your techniques using swatches and different yarns and don't be afraid to take a few risks. There is always a bit of trial and error when dyeing, bleaching or painting your handknits. Embrace the outcome and allow yourself to create freely without inhibition.

DYE

Rit dye is my favorite dye to work with. Rit All-Purpose Dye works best with natural fibers like cotton, wool, linen and silk. It's inexpensive, easy to find and available as a liquid concentrate or powder. Rit also has a dye called Rit DyeMore for Synthetic Fibers that will dye yarn made of synthetic fibers like polyester, polyester-cotton blends, nylon and acrylic. Use Rit DyeMore if you are using yarn with any amount of synthetic fiber.

Your first step will be test-dyeing to make sure you like the end result. The intensity of the color will vary depending on the fiber content, amount of dye used, water temperature and time spent in the dye bath. Before you knit your garment, knit several swatches using the yarn of your choice (or a few different yarns) and dye the swatches to see how each one absorbs the color and how it will look after it's been rinsed and dried.

Adding salt or white vinegar to your dye bath will help intensify the color. If you are using a cotton or linen yarn, add salt. If you are using wool or silk, add white vinegar. I'll talk more about the amounts/ratios below.

So you're ready to dye! Please read all of the steps below before you begin. Take your time, be patient with this process and don't rush through it. First, gather your supplies and prep your work space. You'll need rubber gloves, clothes that you don't mind potentially

staining, an empty 1-gallon milk jug, a measuring cup, salt and/or vinegar, dish soap, something to stir with, one or two old bath towels, a large bucket or stainless steel pot, a large mixing bowl, your swatches and a sink. Wear rubber gloves and have all your supplies ready to go. Cover your work area well or work outside.

NATURAL FIBERS– RIT ALL-PURPOSE DYE

It's time to prepare your dye bath. You can use a large bucket, bowl or pot. To determine how much dye is needed, weigh the garment on a food scale or estimate the weight. As a general guideline, one bottle (or two boxes) of Rit plus 3 gallons of the hottest water safe for your fabric will color up to two pounds of dry weight fabric. Hot water can cause wool to felt, so use warm water with wool and try not to agitate it too much. Add one teaspoon of liquid dish soap to the dye bath. To achieve a darker, more intense color, double the amount of dye. Then add 1 cup of salt to dye bath for cotton or linen, or 1 cup of white vinegar if you are using wool or silk. Stir well.

Wet fabric dyes best, so fill a mixing bowl or bucket with cold water and submerge your swatch/garment. After it's saturated, remove

it from the water and gently wring it out. You can dip the entire garment into the dye, or you can leave a portion of the garment out if you want it to remain the original color. If you are dip/ombre dyeing, you will want to decide which end of your garment will go into the dye and which end will stay out. With your rubber gloves, get a good grip on the section of your garment that you don't want to dye; anything that touches the dye will absorb color very quickly so take care not to let go or drop any part of it. For the dip-dyed sweaters in this book, I connected the ends of the sleeves to the bottom hem of the sweater with removable stitch markers. This made it easier to get an even 'dip' on the whole garment and kept the sleeves in place. To get an ombre effect, let the bottom of the garment stay submerged in the dye, then dip using a slow, smooth motion until the middle of your garment is the desired shade. The water in your saturated garment will help the gradient/ombre absorb smoothly. Let the bottom of your garment soak until you've achieved your desired results.

Still wearing gloves, remove garment from the dye bath and gently wring out the excess dye. Holding the lightest end of your garment at the top (so the dye from the darkest end doesn't dye your light

portion) rinse the entire garment under cool water. Continue rinsing until the water runs clear. Carefully squeeze out excess water and lay garment on an old bath towel. Roll up the towel like a burrito with your garment inside and push down on it with your hands and knees to help remove excess water. Lay out your garment on a blocking surface, reshape and let air dry. (If you are using wool, never put your garment in the dryer. It can felt and/or shrink.)

SYNTHETIC FIBERS- RIT DYEMORE

Rit DyeMore is a synthetic dye that works best on 100% polyester, acrylic, acetate, nylon and polyester/cotton blends. Dyeing on your stove top is recommended when dyeing polyester and acrylic, because a very high temperature is needed to dye these fabrics.

To determine how much dye is needed, weigh the item on a food scale or estimate the weight. One bottle of Rit DyeMore plus 3 gallons of water will dye up to two pounds of dry weight fabric. For very dark colors, we recommend using more dye.

When dyeing synthetic fabrics, always use the stove top method of dyeing. This will ensure a high, steady temperature (about 180F or just below boiling), which is needed to dye synthetics. Fill cook pot with 3 gallons hot tap water. Cover pot and heat water to almost boiling.

When water begins to simmer, add one bottle of DyeMore (shake bottle before pouring) and one teaspoon of dish washing liquid. Stir well with a large spoon.

Wearing rubber gloves, immerse wet garment in dye bath. Stir slowly and continuously for 30 minutes (the first 10 minutes are the most critical). Use tongs to help move the fabric around. Stirring helps to ensure an even color with no splotches. Keep temperature at a low simmer. Item can remain in dye bath for up to one hour. When dyeing polyester, keeping the fabric in the dye bath for at least 30 minutes is essential for ensuring that the color takes fully and does not wash out when rinsed, even if fabric appears to have reached the desired color in less time.

When satisfied with the color, remove the item from the dye bath. The color will appear lighter when dry. Squeeze out excess dye. Rinse item in warm water, then gradually cooler water until water begins to run clear. Then wash in warm, soapy water and rinse. Carefully squeeze out excess water and lay garment on an old bath towel. Roll up the towel like a burrito with your garment inside and push down on it with your hands and knees to help remove excess water. Lay out your garment on a blocking surface, reshape and let air dry.

Visit the links below for fantastic dyeing tutorial videos by Rit Dye.

Shibori dye - https://www.ritstudio.com/2017/02/09/velvet-shibori-pillows/

Ombre dye - https://www.ritstudio.com/techniques/creative-techniques/ombre/

Visit www.ritdye.com for detailed dyeing instructions and a library of over 500 color recipes.

BLEACH

Using bleach to create white spots on fabric is extremely fun and satisfying. I used regular liquid bleach for the projects in this book; I also experimented with bleach pens but they did not yield the same results. Bleach works best on 100% cotton yarn, but you can experiment to see what works for you. When I was envisioning projects for this book, I really hoped to find a black yarn that would bleach completely white. I was only able to find one yarn that could do that – Rowan Original Denim. (All three shades of this yarn will turn white with bleach.) Most of the black cotton yarns I tried to bleach would turn orange or pink. This can look cool too but I

really loved the contrast between the black and white, so I stuck with Rowan Denim. Definitely experiment with yarns before you knit and bleach. Do not attempt to use bleach on wool, silk or mohair.

When you're ready to bleach, test a few swatches first to see what your outcome will be. Cover your work area well and wear clothing that you don't mind potentially bleaching. You may want to wear old jeans – bleach splatters can be a fun addition – or white clothing. Gather a few tools - a measuring cup, paintbrush, toothbrush, spray bottle, squeeze bottle or anything else you might want to use to splatter or drip the bleach on your fabric. Practice splattering and dripping the bleach on your swatch.

In my experience, dry fabric bleaches best. If you're bleaching a sweater or a hat, bunch up old newspapers or plastic bags and stuff them inside to prevent the bleach from soaking through to the other side of your garment. Work on one side of your garment at a time. Lay out your garment on your covered work surface and pour 1/2 cup of bleach into a measuring cup. Use your tools to splash, splatter and drip bleach wherever you'd like. Work a little at a time, then stop and wait for about 5-10 minutes while the bleached areas become more visible. You can always add more bleach later but you can't go back once you've splashed too much on (although bleach always ends up looking pretty cool no matter what.) Let the bleached fabric sit for approximately 30-45 minutes. Once your bleached areas have turned white and you are satisfied with your results, wash garment very thoroughly in cold water to remove the bleach. If you'd like, you can also run it through the washing machine in a small load by itself. Lay your garment out on a blocking surface, reshape and let air dry.

FABRIC PAINT

For the projects in this book I used both white and black Tulip Soft Matte Fabric Paint, which can be found in most craft stores. This paint is available in a wide range of colors and 7 finishes including matte,

neon, pearl, glitter, blow, metallic and velveteen. Tulip also makes a fabric spray paint, which is really fun to use and creates an ombre effect easily.

Before you use fabric paint, experiment on a swatch or two to ensure you like the final result. Cover your work space and gather your materials – fabric paint, paintbrushes, a paint tray and newspapers or something to cover your surface. Lay your garment out and place cardboard or some kind of barrier on the inside (if you are working on a sweater or hat) to prevent paint from soaking through to the other side. Work on one side of your garment at a time and allow the paint plenty of time to dry before working on the other side.

I used the bristles of a medium-sized flat paintbrush to 'stamp' fabric paint on a sweater to create a patterned fabric. You can use also actual stamps or cut your own out of a sponge or piece of foam. Pour some fabric paint into a small tray and use a paintbrush to apply an even coat of paint to your stamp. It's okay if each stamped image isn't perfect – they don't all have to be perfectly even or look exactly the same. I also splattered fabric paint and used a paint brush to paint words. There are so many possibilities - you can do anything you want.

WASHING/CARE INSTRUCTIONS

As with any handknit item, you will want to treat your dyed, bleached and painted garments with care. I don't typically wash most of my handknits but I do like to give them a good soak in wool wash from time to time. Cotton accessories/garments that are bleached can be washed and then air-dried without any issues. But I most likely won't be throwing my hand-painted sweater in the washing machine. Fabric paint will survive a good soak or spot-clean. And the sweaters that were dip-dyed in black dye can be soaked as well. Always check the label on your yarn for care instructions and if you follow them, your dyed, bleached or hand painted garment should be just fine.

KNITTING TECHNIQUES

LONG-TAIL CAST ON

Begin with a long tail, roughly three times the width of your finished piece of knitting. Leaving your estimated length of yarn for the long tail, make a slip knot. Place the slip knot on one needle and gently pull the yarn tails to tighten. Hold needle in your right hand with the tip of the needle pointing to the left. Using your left hand, grasp the two yarn ends below the slip knot. With your left thumb pressing against your left forefinger, move your thumb and forefinger through the space between the two strands. The long tail should be lying over your thumb and the working yarn over your forefinger. Spread your thumb and forefinger apart and lower the needle so that the yarn makes a V between the thumb and forefinger. Hold both tails tightly against your palm with your ring and pinky finger. With the needle in your right hand, pass the needle under the yarn around the thumb, over the top of the yarn around the forefinger, and back through the yarn around the thumb. Pull the thumb out from the yarn loop and pull gently on the yarn tails to tighten stitch. Repeat these steps until you have cast on the required number of stitches.

PICKING UP STITCHES

Slide knitting needle into an existing stitch, then slide your other needle underneath (into the stitch as if to knit.) Pull the stitch through. You now have a new stitch on your needle. Repeat until you have picked up the number of stitches specified in the pattern.

MATTRESS STITCH – VERTICAL

Thread yarn 3 to 4 times the length of your finished edge onto a tapestry needle. Lay pieces to be sewn flat with edges next to each other, with the right sides facing you. Line up the rows/stitches. Insert a tapestry needle between the first and second stitches in the first row. Slide the tapestry needle under two rows, then bring it back to the front between the first and second stitch of the row. Starting on the opposite end, work under two rows again and repeat, zig-zagging from side to side. Stitch under the strands that correspond directly to the other side without skipping rows. Keep the seam elastic by working loosely, then pulling seam stitches gently after working a few inches.

SHOULDER SEAM STITCH – STOCKINETTE

With right sides facing you, thread the yarn onto a tapestry needle. Insert the needle from back to front into the middle of the V of the first stitch on the right edge of the knitting. Pull yarn through. On the opposite side of the knitting, work from the right edge and the front side of the work. Insert the tapestry needle behind the two legs of the first stitch. Pull yarn through. Repeat this step, inserting needle under the legs of the stitches on each side of the work. Try to match the tension of the seam to the tension of your knitting.

ACKNOWLEDGEMENTS

I would like to personally thank the following people for their support in the making of this book:

Thank you Joelle Blanchard for being the brightest and very best at making my ideas come alive. You are a dream. Thank you Stefanie Goodwin-Ritter for being the most fantastic tech editor in the universe. Thank you Armin Trepic and Nyayop Chuol Toang for making this book beautiful. Thank you Erin Hogan for always being willing to look over my grammar and punctuation in exchange for dinner at Orlondo's. Thank you Emily Elliott for walking alongside me through this process every damn time. Thank you Nichole McDowell for your lightning-fast knitting fingers. Thank you Steven Berg, Missy Ridley and the entire StevenBe family for being the coolest, always. Thank you to my knitting gang – Emily, Nichole, Taylor, Melissa, Sarah, Jenni, Josh, Darcy, Alexis, Nikki, Heidi, Amanda, Amy and Robyn. I love and appreciate you guys more than words can say. Thank you Gaye Gillespie/GGMadeIt – love you. Thank you Purl Soho and Cassandra Thoreson for all of your support. Thank you Knitting Next Door. Thank you Nina Chicago. Thank you NIN and Grimes.

Thank you Björk. (Thank you.) Thank you Alanis. Thank you India, thank you terror. Thank you disillusionment. Thank you frailty, thank you consequence. Thank you, thank you silence. Thank you Mom, Dad, Karen, Chris and the fam supporting all my weird hobbies and allowing me to hide out in my room to draw, paint and listen to music when I was a kid. Thank you internet friends, far and wide, who have been there all along with support and words of encouragement via the magical world of blogs, emails, Instagram photos, Ravelry projects and Facebook groups. A huge thank you to Ewe Ewe Yarns, Knit Safari, Loopy Mango, Madelinetosh, Rowan Yarns, Shibui, Third Piece, Spud & Chloë by Blue Sky Fibers and Wool and the Gang for your beautiful yarn. And last but not least, thank you to my awesomely wild and wonderful family: Bo, Lotus and Bowie. I could not follow my dreams and manage to write a book without your sweet faces in my life every day. You put the smile on my face and the beat in my heart. I love you more than knitting.

AT A GLANCE

WINDOWS
RAGLAN PULLOVER SWEATER
PAGE 96

POLAR
SUPER BULKY THROW
PAGE 101

BLEACH
SHAWL/BANDANA
PAGE 103

GLACIER
RAGLAN PULLOVER SWEATER
PAGE 104

SPACE
COWL
PAGE 113

LINK
COWL
PAGE 114

ASH
RAGLAN PULLOVER SWEATER
PAGE 116

CLOUD
SUPER SCARF
PAGE 121

HUNTER
COWL
PAGE 107

HALO
COWL/WRAP
PAGE 108

TWIG
HAT
PAGE 110

ECHO
COWL
PAGE 112

CALIFORNIA
HAT
PAGE 122

VENICE
HAT
PAGE 124

REBEL
TANK
PAGE 126

ABOUT THE AUTHOR

Jen Geigley lives, knits and creates in Des Moines, Iowa with her husband and two children. Known for her clean, modern designs, Jen has an appreciation for simple knits that are easy to wear. Her designs have been published in *Vogue Knitting Magazine, Knit Simple Magazine, Noro Magazine, Knitsy Magazine, Love of Knitting Magazine*, Rowan's *Online Publications* and she has self-published knitwear patterns on Ravelry since 2010. She has written and self-published *Weekend: Simple, Modern Knits* and *Everyday: A Casual, Modern Hand-Knit Collection*. Jen is passionate about sharing her love of knitting by teaching knitting classes to adults and children at local schools and workshops and loves to knit with her daughter. Originally trained in the arts, she creates her own sketches, illustrations, schematics and graphic design work. In her spare time, she enjoys watching Quentin Tarantino movies, traveling, going to concerts and listening to all kinds of music.

Website: www.jengeigley.com
Blog: www.heyjenrenee.com

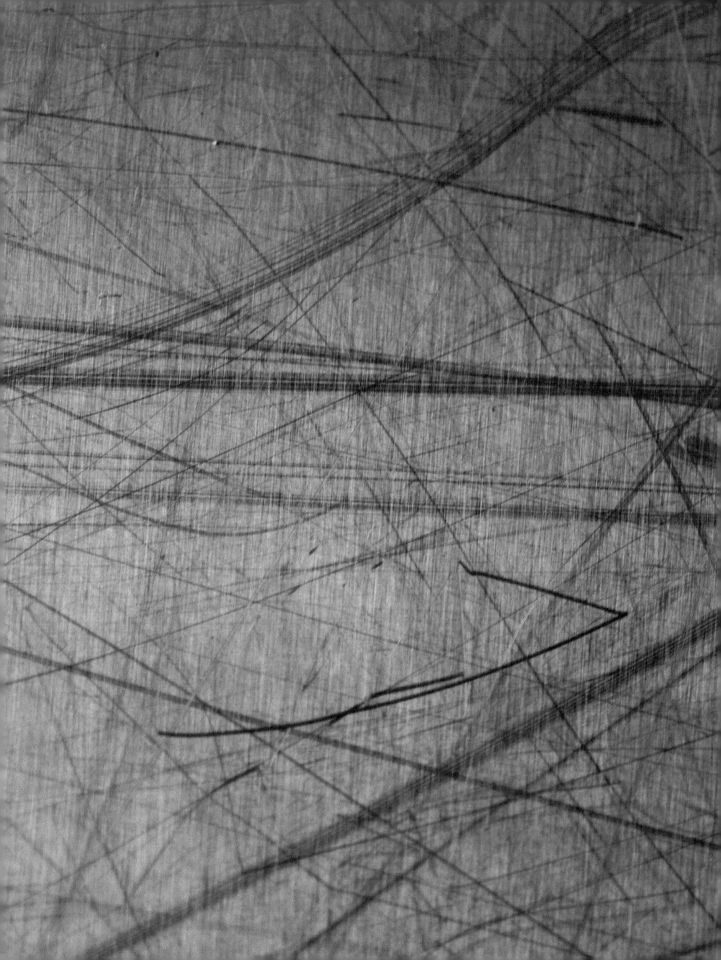

CPSIA information can be obtained
at www.ICGtesting.com
Printed in the USA
LVHW07n1720090718
583161LV00014B/174/P